FROM CRACK TO CHRIST

THE UNTOLD TRUTH AND TESTIMONY OF CHERIESE FOSTER

CHERIESE FOSTER

St. Elite Publishing

CONTENTS

Shirley LaTour, support@slelitepublishing.com

Publisher: SL Elite Publishing

451-D East Central Texas Expy

Suite 276

Harker Heights, TX 76548

From Crack to Christ may be purchased at special quantity discounts. Resale opportunities are available for donor programs, fund raising, book clubs, or other educational purposes for schools. For more information contact: Shirley LaTour at www.slelitepublishing.com or Cheriese Foster at mrscherieseking@gmail.com.

ISBN (Paperback): 978-1-950289-28-8
ISBN (EBook): 978-1-950289-29-5
Author: Cheriese Foster

I dedicate this book to anyone who is suffering with trauma, addictions, or abuse.

DISCLAIMER: This document contains recollections of the author as best perceived and remembered. It may contain shocking realizations and portrayals that may be triggering. Please be advised that the information expressed is intended to be an informal personal testimony, as told in her own cultural voice.

ADDICTION

"Addiction is a psychological and physical inability to stop consuming a chemical, drug, activity, or substance, even though it is causing psychological and physical harm."

Felman, A. (2018, October 26). "What is addiction?" *Medical News Today*. Retrieved from https://www.medicalnewstoday.com/articles/323465.php.

He Had Another Plan

If you are reading this book either it's because you have suffered or are suffering from addiction and are looking for a way out, want to continue your journey of sobriety, or you have a family member that is an addict.

I am the little sister who is eight (8) years younger than Cheriese. I am the little sister who as a child, admired her big sister until I was the age of 6. At the tender age of 6, I remember being so excited to go Christmas shopping with my big sister without any adults.

We went to the mall and I remember her asking me what I wanted. I showed her a sweatshirt that I liked. I can remember what it looked like so vividly.

Cheriese then asked me to turn around and watch out for people. I didn't know what she was doing at first, so I turned my back.

I was heartbroken and terrified when I realized she was stealing the shirt. I was shaking all the way out the store and the entire ride home. My dad asked me how my day went upon returning home and I wanted so badly to tell him what happened; but, I didn't want to be a rat or snitch. After that time I refused to go anywhere else with Cheriese without an adult.

That was pretty early in her teenage years, I watched her go from stealing, to always getting in trouble for being disrespectful, fighting at school, being with older men, in and out of jail, and becoming addicted to crack cocaine. I would go months without seeing Cheriese and would feel relief when my dad would tell me she was in jail.

I can recall a night being home from college laying on the couch watching the news. The news reported that they had found a woman beaten, raped outside of a church and found frozen. They flashed a picture on the TV and said the woman's name, which was Cheriese Foster, my big sister.

I immediately jumped up and called my father. He had already been at the hospital to see Cheriese and didn't know if she was going to make it, but she did. I just knew this was going to be the thing to get her clean. She came home and lived with my dad for a few months and healed up, she said she was going into a program, but then one day she left and never came back.

I was heartbroken again, and after that I didn't see my sister for over 15 years. I would pray for her everyday but at the same time braced myself for that call that would say she had been killed. But God, He had another plan for her life.

So, as you're reading this book, just know that I understand that addiction is a disease that doesn't just affect the one who's using, but the entire family.

After seeing Cheriese's transformation my faith has gotten stronger. What I've learned through this turning point is that life and death are in the power of the tongue. So speak life into your situation or life into your loved one and watch how God moves.

LaShannon Foster

INTRODUCTION

A lot of people don't understand addiction, they don't believe that addiction is a disease. They are ignorant of the word "addiction". Addicts' lives matter indeed! We are one of the smartest human beings on Earth. An addict will go over and beyond to meet any needs that they have. We are not born in addiction; this is a way of filling a "void."

My addiction started with the abuse from childhood, while others either saw their siblings, parents, or other older adults using drugs and other mind-altering substances.

The hurt, betrayal, and for the most part curiosity, lead me to use drugs. I felt comfort whenever I drank and got high off of drugs, not realizing at the time that the problems were still there or recurred shortly after my usage. The drugs blocked my feelings and replaced them with the euphoria.

EUPHORIA: an exaggerated feeling of physical and mental well-being, especially when not justified by external reality (https://medical-dictionary).

I felt great until the drugs wore off, and I was exhausted the morning after drinking alcohol.

Now I understand what I didn't understand before. When problems and issues occur, I relax my mind with prayer and meditation or soft gospel music. I uplift my spirit by praising My God. He is the only way I know how to defeat any mental issue, traumatic situation, or negative feeling I may be experiencing at the time.

I tell you this to say only one thing. God is a waymaker, a sponsor, a healer, a teacher, a parent and a best friend. Turn to Him. Ask, and you shall receive. He will work in your life if you just call on Him. Ask Him to prove His existence. He will, I am a witness!

EARLY SCHOOL DAYS

*O*ld Trail School in Bath, Ohio was where my elementary education began. A girl named "Amanda" became my best friend at school. The teachers and principal were so very kind. The students were very friendly. During recess, there was lots of fun and laughter on the playground. I enjoyed the experience at Boston Mills Ski Resort; especially spelling, swimming, and skiing. It was one of the many extra activities afforded to us at this private school. I was happy as anyone could be and really looked forward to school days.

I was a happy, quiet, and polite little girl who had one neighborhood friend. For no apparent reason, this friend for some reason decided to fight me one day, and I ran home crying. The next day, mom bought me a book about friendships. Inside she wrote, "Know who your real friends are". At that moment my dog, Caesar, became my best friend. I played solo. Some people would agree that this was normal.

Mom and I had deep conversations. Back then we were all we had. We talked about how different my new friends were from the old neighborhood and how I loved being around my friends at Old Trail. Mom and Caesar were my best friends.

After our talk about friendship, suddenly there was a loud noise. The door flew open and a strange man was standing there. Mom was calm, as usual.

She said to the stranger, "You have three minutes to get off my porch, and two of those minutes are gone."

The man said, "Oh, you'll call the police?"

Mom said, "No, I'll be calling you an ambulance in less than one minute." Mom was nothing to play with. She was what you would consider an intelligent and educated "OG". She had many college degrees. I felt safest with mom.

I attended another elementary school in West Akron before finally arriving at Perkins Middle School. Boy, was this school a shock compared to previous schools. It was a completely different environment. The people who attended Perkins were not kind or friendly, as I had experienced at my private school.

They seemed to think that they were "all that." They dressed up-to-date and, me, well, I was used to always wearing uniforms so I didn't have many clothes but I stayed neat. The students' attitudes were different, and they were stuck up and ghetto af! Most importantly, there were student bullies. I didn't really feel like I fit in at Perkins.

My mom started fostering children at this time and I wasn't ok with it; but I was sort of glad they were around. Man, could they fight. I was somewhat of a timid person, certainly not a fighter (then). Some of the bullies attended Perkins and I was terrified because some of them targeted me for some reason. They really didn't like me at all; perhaps because I was quiet, spoke "proper English," or because I was well dressed and groomed.

I guess they wondered what "hood" I came from. LOL. They claimed I was a white girl trapped in a black girl's body. Huh, maybe so. One particular bully named "C", along with her two sidekick friends, mocked the way I talked; because of private schools, I spoke very proper English.

One day, they followed me home from school. I rushed into the house, told my mom what was going on, and started crying. We had a long talk that day. The very next day, the same thing happened. I ran toward home and the three bullies chased me. I ran track and was the second fastest student on the track team … I ran up on the porch but this time the screen door was locked.

"Dammit Ma!" I yelled.

My mom stood inside the doorway and calmly said, "Bullying stops today!"

With that being said, she opened the screen door and my two older, bigger, and tougher foster sisters came outside; maybe to make sure the ensuing fight was fair.

Mom then said, "Hit that big mouthy one!"

I went back into the yard, scared to death, and started swinging—hard and fast. I didn't really know that I had it in me, but I should have known because my parents were not pushovers when fighting was necessary.

My parents were "Beasts " with their hands, especially my mom. Her hands were registered by the State. She was a black belt in Taekwondo. My dad was a knockout artist in his younger days too; I would soon learn I had the fighting instinct in me all along, with multiple personalities.

As it turned out, I won the fight. The very next day at school everyone was "kissing my butt". Even the main bully's two friends wanted to now be friends with me. From that day on, I had no more trouble at school with bullies. When the weather was nice, my sisters and I walked to and from school together to make sure that there were no more problems. We had strict instructions from mom, "Don't ever, ever start trouble!"

My attitude began to change after the fight with the main bully, and after I started hanging out with the "cool girls". Troublemakers.

Whatever was going on with my attitude, I always did my school work and respected teachers and other school personnel, as I had been raised. Occasionally, however, I caused a ruckus. I had trouble with a girl named "JQ".

She got on my last nerve one day, so I beat her up badly. Her mother pressed charges against me. I had broken her jaw. No more modeling for her for a while. And I'll bet she'll think twice about liking the same boy I liked.

It was rumored that some of JQ's family members were planning to "get even" and beat me up the next day after school. That same night, I stole a gun from my grandaddy and put it in my bookbag. I was ready for whatever happened the next day in school. As it turned out, someone had snitched on me about the gun.

The principal raided my locker, found the gun, and I was expelled. (My dad and I went fishing often and I remembered his comment, "A fish cannot be caught if its mouth is closed"). I should've kept my big mouth shut about having the gun in my locker.

Eventually, I was bussed to Innes Junior High School in Ellet and sometime thereafter became a statistic, a 9th grade dropout.

OVERCOMING AFFLICTION

*T*hat man came into my room late that night with the stench of alcohol on his breath. I closed my eyes tight to pretend I was asleep until I felt the hot sweat from his curly chest hairs on my frail body, soaking up my nightgown.

This was that same man that helped raise me, that same man that said he loved me, that same man that was now beginning to grind his way into a climax on top of me. The same man that vowed to love my grandmother until death. That man was my grandmother's husband. I called him "granddaddy".

I would lay there and pray to God, a God I was told would protect me from harm. The truth is, I didn't blame God; I blamed myself for being sicker than the man who was molesting me. I loved the rides on his shoulders and back. I loved the attention of being accepted.

He spoke words of encouragement to me daily, he also reminded me of how beautiful my smile was and how nice I looked before school. I loved it! Who was sicker? Me or him?

The touching had gotten worse. I needed some relief. I began cutting on my upper arms and legs. The more I cut, the better I felt and dealt with the sexual abuse I was now experiencing. I cut long and deep until I felt the warmth of blood trickle down my arms and legs. The more blood I saw, the more relieved I felt. It was a feeling of freedom. I loved the feeling of "freedom"; it was my safe place.

I would go to school everyday, a seemingly "normal student". I attended Our Lady of The Elms, a private school. My grades began to drop from straight A's down to C's and D's. It was immediately detected. I was put into counseling at Child Guidance just to be told I suffered from depression and other mental illness issues.

Now, what does a 10-year-old girl know about depression? And how in the hell was this a mental defect? I would always wish they had just asked me if anyone was hurting me. The question never came about. I mutilated my body until my early adulthood when granddaddy finally died. The most confusing part of it all is, I actually miss this man.

I missed the attention and money he gave me as I had grown older. By that time, I had learned to use what I had to get what I wanted (Another way of admitting to prostituting myself.) which came in handy later on in life.

I had developed a codependent relationship with my grandfather, and now he was gone. I wanted to believe he died of guilt, but doctors said it was cancer. I still call it "karma".

Shortly afterward, I became dependent on alcohol and drugs. I found the absent love in a few bottles a day. Now I bet you're wondering where my parents were?

My mother thought I was in good hands living with my grandparents, so there was never an issue, little did she know...My father was out doing his own thing with the ladies. All I had was my grandma, and I refused to tell her I was deeply in love with her husband, my grandfather.

Rewinding the moment of time when I fell in love with my own grandfather ...... He was officially my enabler, but, I called him, "my trick." As I grew deeper into my early addiction, he'd sneak and hand me fifty-dollar bills.

. . .

I loved being in control of his sick fetish as well as my own. I knew what made him squirm. I watched his eyes follow me around the house when I wore those tight, pink jeans he liked so much. It caught his attention every time. My granny would say, "Take those tight pants off!"

My alcohol addiction started pulling double shifts. My mind and actions had become so conniving and scandalous. I knew the blackmail game oh so well now. The more my addiction grew, and the older I got, my body was no longer a temple but a way to con men out of money and I used it to my advantage.

I was now 17, a full-blown crack addict. Smoking crack was my ultimate release of sick secrets I kept buried inside of me, another safe place. My addiction had gotten worse by the second and led me to a life of crime. Shit got real, real fast…....

JUVENILE DELINQUENT

*L*et's go back to an either time when I was 14: I ran away from home for the first time in October 1987 and subsequently began a journey through Summit County Juvenile Court. My offense was being unruly, and I confessed to the charge.

The referee said I had to continue going to the Child Guidance Center for counseling, obey all laws, and parents' rules. Furthermore, I was threatened with being locked up in the detention home if there were any more complaints. About a month later, I ran away again and didn't resurface until January 1988. Back to court I went. A review of my case was set for March 14, 1988.

I did pretty good for a while but was charged with violating a court order on March 4, 1989. It was on my dad's birthday. LOL. The charge was a probation violation, runaway.

A warrant was issued for my arrest and detention pending a hearing which was held a couple weeks later. Yes, I had violated probation by being AWOL from home. Yes, I was found to be delinquent.

Yes, I think I stayed in the detention home for four or five days. And yes, back to Child Guidance I went, where the social worker recommended some kind of program. My case was set to close on May 31, 1988, if there were no new offenses. I did pretty good for a while.

During this time, I started dating "Craig" who was 21 years old. Since he looked younger, we lied about his age. Craig taught me how to drive a car, a Cutlass. I drove around town with loud music bumping, drinking alcohol, and smoking weed regularly.

After quite a while, my dad discovered the truth about Craig's age and threatened him, big time! Dad's discovery marked the end of my relationship with Craig. I wasn't too happy because the fun had come to an end.

On January 14, 1989, I was arrested for stealing from the Higbee department store which was then located in Rolling Acres Mall. The value of the stolen goods was $59.98. I was detained in the detention home pending release on February 10th. Yes, I admitted guilt and a hearing was set for February 7th.

My dad, maternal grandmother, a children's services caseworker, and I were at the hearing. The probation officer had to decide if I should be released to children's services or to a relative. It was recommended that I have psychological testing. Finally, on May 12th, my dad and I met with the probation officer.

My probation for the department store theft was terminated; case closed. Things did not improve after the probation was terminated. Later that year, on September 7th, my dad filed an unruly complaint in juvenile court claiming that I was delinquent "by reason of incorrigibility".

A hearing was set for September 25th. I didn't show up and was on the run again. After resurfacing, I was placed on probation and stayed in detention until October 2nd.

A review of this case was set for December 18th. However, one day before closing my case, the probation officer reported me AWOL from home, chronic truancy from school, and suspension from school for failure to serve a 10-day suspension.

. . .

A hearing was set for June 20, 1990. The probation officer recommended dismissal of probation violation and terminated my probation. She also said that my case could be sealed on September 7, 1991 if there were no new offenses.

Unfortunately, on February 1, 1991, I got another unruly case for curfew violation. This time the charge was filed by the Akron Police Department. A police officer stopped me because, as a minor, I was not supposed to be out on the streets without an adult between 11:00 pm and 5:00 am.

A hearing was set for February 25th. By this time, I was 18 years old as of February 2, 1991. I was too old for Juvenile Court and too old for the detention home. Besides this, my whereabouts were unknown to whoever might be looking for me. I was grown; so, I said goodbye to Summit County Juvenile Court, judges, referees, probation officers, and my parents.

PHYSICALLY/EMOTIONALLY TORN

*I*n my later teenage years, I started dating a man named "Dee". He was physically abusive. He blacked my eye and busted my lip. He was also emotionally abusive. Sometimes, he would embarrass me while we were out together in public.

I didn't tell anyone about the abuse. Instead, I lied about injuries and said I had been fighting. At some point, I moved in with Dee. He really thought he owned me then. He controlled the way I dressed and where I went, even the friends I could hang with.

He sold crack cocaine. Some of his crackhead customers came where we lived and smoked crack. One day, Dee left me with the crackheads while he went to take care of business. One of the crackheads offered me some crack. I refused, preferring to stick with drinking alcohol and smoking weed.

One day, Dee beat me up really bad and told me to get a job. I managed to get hired by two jobs; a nurse aide position and house cleaning. I was terrified of Dee. He was very insecure and violent. He blacked both my eyes, busted my lip, and dragged me down a whole flight of stairs.

Later that night, I planned to escape. I could not and would not take the abuse any more. I thought to myself, "I'm too good and too smart for this shit." I knew for sure that the abuse had nothing to do with love.

My parents loved me and never beat me. I don't ever remember getting a whipping from my parents, much less a beating. I said to myself, "I'm getting out of here." So, I put my clothes in a trash bag and pretended to be taking out the trash.

Later, I called my dad, told him what happened, and said I was ready to come back home. He arrived in less than ten minutes to pick me up and wanted to shoot Dee. I said, "Forget about it; just leave it alone."

With encouragement from my grandmother, I finished nurse's aide training, got certified, and got a job at Valley View Nursing Home. I did really good for a while; things were going great. I was back home with my grandmother, state certified and all. I kept that job for about two (2) years, but got caught up in my past unruly activities. The gun incident was finally brought to court and I was sentenced to 6 months to a year in a place called Brinkhaven.

THE BRINKHAVEN NIGHTMARE

$\mathcal{I}$ was an incorrigible teenager who was finally shipped off to Brinkhaven, a home for troubled and delinquent girls. This "home" was actually a farm. Upon arrival, the very first noticeable thing was the strong smell of manure. Later, I noticed that some girls had empty facial expressions. Brinkhaven turned out to be a hell hole, an evil place.

I didn't sleep very well at night. The more I stayed awake, the more I witnessed girls being taken from their beds and returning hours later with gifts. I guessed these girls were being sexually abused and rewarded with gifts and extra privileges to keep their mouths' shut.

A girl named "Stacy" became my best friend. She was a victim of sexual abuse and confirmed my suspicions about what was going on behind the scenes at Brinkhaven.

One night, Mr. "B" came into my room in the middle of the night and ordered me to come with him. I refused to cooperate. So, I was immediately snatched out of bed, hauled off to the barn, and locked up with some pigs. Boy, that barn really stunk so badly.

It was really dark inside that barn. I began feeling around on the walls, trying to locate a window; there were none. Instead, I felt some farm tools and wrapped my hands around a pitch fork. I sat down on a bundle of hay and began to cry while clutching the pitch fork. All of a sudden, I heard a disgusting pig oinking its way closer to me.

Panic took control of my entire being while I started swinging the pitch fork. A loud agonizing squeal came from the pig's mouth. I screamed! The barn yard door swung open and flashlights blinded me.

I was grabbed and rushed out of the barn, and into a bathroom. There, I was ordered to strip and bathe. Afterwards, the employee warned that I would regret what had happened in the barn.

I was given a toothbrush, ordered to kneel, and scrub the kitchen floor, square by square. Sometimes I laid in bed at night and pretended to be somewhere else. I struggled to get a good night's sleep and wondered if I would be hauled out of bed again. Perhaps I was a little too stubborn for their asses.

Once again, survival skills kicked in. I scoped out the farm's perimeter and started planning to escape. Yes, I was going to escape. Stacy and "Melanie" decided to escape with me. Melanie had it really bad at Brinkhaven. She was abused the most by Mr. B.

A lady employee who worked nights was on our team. She knew what was going on with the abuse and tried to help as best as she could without losing her job. She gave us directions to Akron and told us the best time to leave the farm. She also packed lunches for us.

We still did not really know how to get to Akron; however, only one thing was certain, we were going to leave Brinkhaven. Any place was better than Brinkhaven. I hated that place.

It was nightfall and we were all ready to escape. Out the door we tiptoed through cow manure and then onto our knees, crawling to avoid being seen. We didn't care one bit about crawling in shit. We made it to the gates, crawled underneath, and were then on the dirt road. Once on the road and out of sight of Brinkhaven, we ran as fast as we could.

The next order of business was to find a vehicle. We saw a bar and the parking lot was full of cars. Someone made the mistake of leaving a vehicle unlocked. Seeing that I dealt with older thugs, I knew how to steal cars. I hot-wired the car and off we went. We ditched the car at Portage Lakes and slept.

We were awakened by ducks quacking. This was the most beautiful scene ever. It was temporary freedom.

The three of us planned to go our separate ways upon arrival in Akron. So, I went to my Aunt "Essie's" where my favorite cousin lived. Upon arrival, I knocked loudly. My cousin opened the door and turned up his nose because of the manure smell on my clothing. I stunk so bad.

I ran some bath water and got into the tub, with a squirt of bubbles while cuz dumped my clothes in the garbage can. I ate some good hot food and went to sleep wearing cuz's clothes. Aunt Essie arrived after work and discovered me asleep on the sofa. She woke me up and told me to call my dad and let him know that I was ok.

I told Aunt Essie that I was not going back to Brinkhaven and told her what was going on at that horrible place. She said I could stay at her house as long as I called my dad. So, I did. Not much later after calling my dad, there was a loud knock at the door by men claiming to be police officers. It was!

I ran and hid in the upstairs closet. There was a secret cubby hole in there that only me and cuz knew about. The police looked right in the closet and didn't have a clue that I was just inches away from eye sight. After the police left, my aunt called my dad and let him have it!

Eventually, I turned myself in and wound up in the detention home. That's where I stayed until my dad came to get me. I told him the details about Brinkhaven but wasn't taken seriously. So, again, nothing was done. Eventually, years later, this hell hole was closed down.

ALCOHOL, DRUGS, AND PROSTITUTION

I began drinking beer at age 10. I was about 16 when I snuck into a bar for the first time. Alcohol allowed me to speak freely about whatever was on my mind.

Alcohol was my drug of choice before crack cocaine came into the picture. It made me a little bit too friendly. I hung around older men, that's where I got most of my money to drink.

My mother used to tell me, "Nothing is free in this world." Now I know what she meant by saying that. Later in life, those older men started offering me money for sex, and it sounds crazy, but I actually became addicted to the lifestyle.

I had my way with men anywhere I went. I always got what I wanted, and in return, gave them what their perverted minds desired. I would get drunk and become disrespectful towards anybody that was around me, family included.

There were times when I went to family parties and women would hide their purses and lock certain doors in their homes. I was the first one kicked off the property after too much to drink. One family member guarded the beer and wine coolers. When I caught on to what was going on, I'd yell, "Fuck yaw'll! I'm outta here!" I left.

My mouth was so ignorant and disrespectful. No one wanted me around while I was under the influence of any mind altering substances. I knew that my welcome was worn out. Alcohol brought the worst out of me.

When I was high or drunk from drinking alcohol, I was very loud and ignorant. When drunk, I wanted to go make money. I called it hustling. Others and the courts called it prostitution.

Everything was for sale when it came to getting money for my addictions. I was addicted to alcohol and the accompanying lifestyle consisting of: robberies, breaking and entering, prostitution, theft, and trappin'.

Crack cocaine was my drug of choice. This illegal drug has many names; i.e., dope, work, or, as

I called it, "fire." Crack is a form of cocaine that has been processed into a crystal hard rock. It comes in many colors including pink, pearly white, beige, and grey when recooked.

One form of consuming crack is called freebasing; that's when you smoke crack out of a pipe. Smoking primos is another form of consuming crack. In this case, the crack is smashed up, mixed with tobacco and/or weed, wrapped in rolling papers, and then smoked.

Whatever the consumption method of this highly addictive drug, the effects are the same; it is a stimulant that affects the body's production of dopamine. And I loved it! Everything about it, especially the ability to be who I wanted without feeling guilty of who I had become.

With this explanation, I started smoking primos in 1991. How did it happen? Well, I started hanging around a dude who sold and smoked primos. Dude and I started living together and he introduced me to them. We smoked primos every day. This dude was my baby daddy. We robbed stores together and got high. Man … we were just like "Bonnie & Clyde".

At some point, I realized that primos weren't enough; so, I started freebasing. I was addicted in less than a month from the first time I inhaled that crack demon. I was on a deadly journey to the point of which I thought I had no return.

In 1992, I got pregnant. You would have thought that I would stop smoking crack and getting drunk. Nope! I got worse! I was fearful, and not because of the pregnancy. I was fearful because I simply could not stop smoking crack cocaine.

I gave birth to a daughter at Akron General Hospital in 1993. I was told that I could not take my baby girl home because traces of cocaine were found in her system. A Summit County children's services caseworker was assigned to my case.

I cried and pleaded to take my baby home to Carpenter Street. The crying and pleading paid off. My daughter and I went home together. I actually tried to comply with staying drug free and being a good mother.

However, after a while, I wanted to get high again. By this time, I had learned to beat the system when it came to dropping urine. I bought clean urine contained in a bottle and inserted the bottle into my vagina.

When I arrived to drop, I went into the bathroom, poured the bottled urine into the issued container and turned in the clean urine. I played the system with clean-purchased urine until my case closed. I no longer had to report and drop urine.

Finally, I was on my own. I had purchased a car, a two-toned blue Cutlass. I dibbled and dabbled with the drug. Money was so plentiful because of my job. Then, another demon surfaced. Cocaine. I started snorting and got crazy. I did the most vicious things to people. I broke in houses, robbed, stole, and prostituted myself for these drugs.

Not only did I have all these addictions, but I was also losing my mind. My mental illness increased tremendously. By this time, the addiction had taken full control. I ended up selling the sound system to my car, then the rims, and eventually the whole car.

During December 1993 or January 1994, my daughter and I moved from the one-bedroom apartment on Carpenter Street into a two-bedroom apartment on Oak Park.. My mother tried to reach me by telephone to see if we needed anything. There was no answer.

During my absence, my mother took my daughter after finding her alone in our apartment. I think she knew what was going on with me and drugs. But I told her my daughter wasn't alone, my neighbor was right downstairs. She just so happened to be my mom's boyfriend's daughter so I thought it was cool to run down the street and grab what I needed to grab and then get back.

From 1994 to 1995, I was working at a nursing home. One day, the Director of Nursing called me to her office and fired me because I had lied on the job application about being a felon. I was heated, pissed off. So, I went home and later made a bomb threat about blowing up the nursing home.

I was charged with making false alarms, put on probation, and given a restraining order to stay 50 feet away from the nursing home. That was the end of my nursing assistant license. My anger issues had skyrocketed. Everything was everybody's fault but my own.

In July 1996, she filed for and was awarded temporary guardianship of my daughter; and later became her guardian for an indefinite time period. Quite frankly, I didn't want my daughter raised in a crack cocaine environment.

At no time did I want her to be affected by what was going on, or to see what was going on. So indeed I did the best thing I could possibly do for my daughter at that time. I knew my mom would raise her to be the bright young lady that later I would know her to be.

In '97-'98, I was pregnant again. While at a trap house, I hit a piece of crack so potent that I went into labor. Somebody called a cab instead of 911 to haul my crackhead-ass out of the trap house. On the way to Akron General Hospital, my water broke and there was lots of moisture. Afterwards, I could feel my baby's little head pressing against my cervix.

For the second time in my life, I was really scared to be in the same hospital again delivering another crack-addicted baby. This time I delivered a son. Ok, round two with children's services and armed with the same game, promising to stay clean of crack cocaine if allowed to keep my son. They did allow me to keep him.

This time, however, I really and truly tried so hard to stay clean of drugs. After six months (9/20/98), I caught a child endangering case for leaving my son alone in the apartment. I was living on East Tallmadge Ave. I didn't lose my son because of drugs…. let me explain just in case my son happens to read this book.

I went outside to beat this girl's ass for ringing my doorbell. There was a do not disturb sign on the door. My son had tremors and I used to sing to him hoping to calm his nerves. So, while feeding, I would sing to him and afterwards rock him to sleep. This was our private and quiet time together.

Anyway, while outside fighting, someone called the police. I was arrested and hauled off to jail. My son went to children's services. Once released from jail, I tried, to no avail, to get my son back. I was heartbroken and felt betrayed. Anger and resentment took over my mind and body. All hope was lost; along with self-respect, morals, dignity, and spirituality.

The only way that I could cope with loss was to get high. So, I was "off to the races" again to smoke crack. I was in full-blown go mode. As my crack addiction worsened, so did my anger issues. I was bitter, as bitter as Satan himself. The hood created an image of me named The Tasmanian Devil or "Taz", my alter ego.

So, Taz resurfaced and rapidly leaped into go mode. After several weeks in go mode, my body was completely worn out. I was tired and could no longer continue at the same pace. I really needed a break from the streets for a while. For sure, I needed help and had to get help again.

That same evening, I left a message for my Community Support Services caseworker. She returned my call the following morning. I returned to the program for more guidance and counseling. Once again, I complied with program requirements.

After completing the program, the caseworker

helped me with getting housing for the fourth time. Eventually, I was granted a housing certificate.

"Congratulations Cheriese," a staffer said.

Little did anyone know that I was on my way to opening another trap house. I couldn't wait to notify the dope boys that a trap house would soon be open for business.

TRAP HOUSES

J began hanging out with the dope boys who sold crack cocaine and other drugs. The dope boys usually operated out of trap houses which were usually apartments that dope boys "took over" in exchange for giving the resident a cut of the drugs or money.

Dope boys were always armed with pistols, mostly because the North Side was full of haters; robbery and shootings were not uncommon. Haters wanted the money that dope boys earned and would not hesitate to rob, steal, and shoot. This scene did not scare me, it was very rare that I feared anything. I had become totally committed to the game.

The next move for me was to allow my apartment to be used as a trap house. Usually, I worked the door in order to keep track of all the money coming in and going out of the house. In this way, I could keep track of profits in order to know how much money was owed to me. I could also "tear a dope boy's mouth out," which meant that I could cheat them out of some crack.

I had one of the biggest trap houses on the North Side while living on Tallmadge Avenue. The dope boys named it "the million dolla' spot" because big money numbers were racked up.

Everyone made money; selling everything from dope to sex to dinners. Drug paraphernalia was also sold. Crack heads bought chore boy and pipes; tricks who came to buy sex also bought condoms. If everything went well, the tricks would pay me because I was the house lady. This was an extra come-up on some dough.

While freebasing, some people would get "noided and geeked" (paranoid), trip out real bad, and then do some weird-ass shit. There was a certain dude who frequented the trap house named "Bug Man". He got this name because every time that mothafucka would hit the crack he got naked thinking that bugs were crawling on his ass.

We, in turn, would go through his pants pockets and take money. Bug Man made the trap house hot when the crack was real good. He made it hot by hollering loudly and running outside naked. Eventually, he was barred from my dope house.

Ultimately, the trap house got real hot and I got evicted. I was also hot and had no money. I couldn't risk catching a case for prostitution, robbery, theft or anything else. Since I was hot and broke, it was impossible to find a place to crash for any length of time.

People in the "hood" were of no value. The dope boys were of less value because they didn't care about me or anyone else getting evicted. Efforts to get some free crack or a couple of dollars for food fell on deaf ears. A typical response for a drug handout was, "This shit ain't free. You better get another spot so we can trap."

Every now and then, dope boys might let you earn a couple pieces of crack by working that neck or moving them hips. The struggle was real and getting more difficult with each passing day.

THE STRUGGLE GETS REAL

I was homeless again so I headed to the shelter. On check day, the first of the month, I cashed my SSI check, blew it on drugs and missed my curfew at the shelter. Kicked out on my ass once again with nowhere to go and having burned all my bridges, I headed back North.

I stayed with a few friends and when I got broke, I was put out but only to return with fire, literally. I was tired of being used so I went out and robbed a man for $7000.00.

I disappeared for at least four (4) months only to return broke with nothing to show but some sneakers, some new clothes, and a little piece of car that I shared with a man who would soon be the one who would later try to kill me……

. . .

Mental Health Issues

I was referred to a place called Community Support Services (CSS). Someone told me that this agency could help me find housing. However, the catch was that I had to become a client and follow the rules of a personalized treatment plan, managed by a caseworker. After being evaluated and diagnosed, I was placed in the Pact Team which is for clients in need of the most help.

I gave the Pact Team caseworker pure hell. Also, I got caught stealing an envelope full of money. It was a client's allowance. Clients receive an allowance out of their monthly checks. I knew how to pop the locked drawer and did just that in order to steal someone's allowance money.

About a year later, I was put on SSI for mental health issues. My brain was literally fried. I heard voices and saw shadows. I bought a gun off the block, went berserk, shot up a N. Howard Street block in broad daylight.

I had literally lost my mind. I often talked to myself and sometimes even answered. My drug use had gotten the best of me. Yeah, I must say the struggle got real. I was put on different kinds of psych meds intended to help stabilize my mental issues.

. . .

While participating in the Pact Team program, I didn't feel as if I was getting any better. All I wanted to do was get the allowance and go get high, so I complied with the program.

Regardless of my addiction issues, the CCS staff were always compassionate towards me and I admired them. I learned to play the system in ways you wouldn't imagine. Things were going great for me, so I thought.

"PYRO"

I was in full blown addiction and suffering from PTSD, anxiety, paranoia, and a vicious fetish called pyromania. According to Encyclopedia of World Problems and Human Potential, Pyromania is an impulse control disorder in which individuals constantly fail to resist their impulses to purposely start fires in order to relieve tension or for instant gratification.

I had become dangerous to myself and others. I would set fires in the woods, small bugs, and much more. I knew setting fires was extremely dangerous but didn't care. I wanted some relief and I needed it bad. …

. . .

WHO SET THE FIRE?

I really don't want to get involved with this story, but just know my mom's house burned down. The detectives say it was arson. Setting fire was one of my fetishes, but just for the record, I am not implicating myself nor am I admitting to having anything to do with the fire at this location. One of the foster children did the time, after she confessed to the crime. Case closed.

In 2020, I also confessed to my mother some things that actually happened that day of the fire. I was taught in the 12-Step program of AA to right my wrongs, make amends, and ask for forgiveness only if it wouldn't put me in harm's way. My mother understood and also told me that she already knew the truth.

I will not go any further in talking about the war stories to protect myself and the fact that I was never charged with any of these acts of rage......

PARANOIA

I was tired of getting high. I wanted out. I didn't really know how I was going to stop this addiction but what I did know is I was damn sure gonna try.

. . .

I would sit in the house at night with a loaded .38 snub nose and be so paranoid. I would sit in the dark with my door open at night, higher than a cloud, and aim my pistol at my screen… I don't know what I thought was going to come through that door but whatever it was, I was ready for it.

My body poured down sweat. My clothes were drenched. I would often go outside to do a perimeter check to make sure my coast was clear.

I hung loud clinging wind chimes on my windows and my doors so I could hear someone come in if I was to fall asleep. I tucked my gun under my pillow with my finger still on the trigger.

At times I had wished it would go off in my sleep and end my misery. I wanted out! Any way possible… and I was ready to turn to just the person (spirit) that would free me…

CRIMINAL RECORD

From 1991 through 1997, I was found guilty of six traffic offenses: driving over a fire hydrant, running a red light, driving an unsafe vehicle, loud muffler, failure to dim, and no driver's license.

In November 1994, I was found guilty of making false alarms. On other occasions, I was charged with aggravated menacing, assault, and resisting arrest. These charges were all dismissed except for resisting arrest of which I was found guilty.

In 1995, I was charged with theft and appeared in Akron Municipal Court. The result was guilty as charged. At the same time as the theft arrest, I was also charged with misrepresenting my identity. This case was dismissed. Later on, I earned a felony which was aggravated burglary. The following narrative describes what happened.

While living on Carpenter Street, this chick who owed me money asked me to watch her apartment while she went to Cleveland for a couple days. I thought, *She has a lot of nerve; going to Cleveland for a couple days and claiming to have no money to pay me.* Nevertheless, I agreed to "keep an eye out."

The more I thought about it, the angrier I got. So, I took the liberty of breaking into the chick's crib, stole money, and dope contained in a shoe box and hidden in a wall. Besides the shoe box, the chick claimed that I stole her entertainment center.

I looked straight into the judge's face and told him exactly what I did: broke into the apartment and stole the shoe box containing money and drugs, but at 120 pounds, I had absolutely nothing to do with removing the entertainment center.

The penalty was 18 months on probation. While on probation in 1996, I was arrested for assault and faced the Judge. Yes, I was guilty as charged.

I was off the radar until 1998 and then caught two theft cases. Nine contempt of court charges are associated because I didn't show up for court. Finally, I showed up and faced Judge #6. You guessed it, guilty as charged. The case closed in

September 1999. No sooner had I caught my breath from the theft episode, I was arrested and charged with endangering children. Seven contempt of court charges are associated; once again, I didn't show up for court. Finally, I appeared before the Judge. You guessed it, guilty as charged. Case closed September 20, 1999.

- 1999: Charged with soliciting, found guilty, Judge #5 case closed October 5, 1999, guilty of one contempt (one was dismissed).
- 1999: Theft charge, found guilty by Judge #5. Case closed October 5, 1999.
- 1999: Drug paraphernalia, dismissed by Judge #5, March 14, 2000.
- 2001: Occupy drug premise, guilty; case closed June 4, 2002, Judge #5; 6 contempt of court charges.

All was quiet on the home front for three years. Then, in 2004, I was arrested and charged with soliciting. Six contempt of court charges associated with this one. I was finally marched to court and faced Judge #4. You guessed it, guilty as charged. This case closed April 6, 2004.

. . .

Also, in 2004, I was arrested and charged with drug
paraphernalia. After eight contempt of court
charges, I showed up for court. The result was
guilty as charged. The case was closed April 6,
2005. Although dismissed, I was also charged at the
same time as the above with marijuana drug abuse,
as well as eight contempt of court charges; the case
was closed April 6, 2005.

- 2005: Charged with criminal trespassing,
  found guilty, Judge #5; case closed June
  29, 2006. Two contempt of court
  charges.
- 2006: Charged with robbery, transferred
  to Summit County Court, 1 contempt
  of court, case closed July 9, 2006. I "was
  granted two years of community control
  (probation) on August 16, 2006 . .
  successfully released from supervision on
  December 31, 2008 after her period of
  supervision had been extended."
- 2007: While on probation, I was
  arrested and charged with drug
  paraphernalia which was dismissed.
  Case closed July 30, 2007. At the same
  time, charged and found guilty of
  criminal trespassing, found guilty by

Judge #6, case closed July 30, 2007, one contempt of court charge.

- 2008: While still on probation, I was arrested again for soliciting, and found guilty by Judge #1; the case closed September 30, 2008. Finally, on December 31, 2008, I was off probation.

- 2012, I caught a case for receiving stolen property, guilty by Judge #1, case closed July 17, 2012, two contempt of court charges dismissed.

FELONY CONVICTION

*R*emember how I said I became pure evil and committed various crimes? Now I will share my first felony conviction which happened in 2006. The charge was robbery in the second degree, and it was my favorite. The following paragraphs detail what happened.

Once upon a time, there was this lame-ass dude named "E" who was a crackhead with a paycheck. He also tricked prostitutes. The hood bitches always tricked with E. As a prostitute, at the time, I didn't trick with E. I couldn't stand him. The word was out that he enjoyed de-humanizing prostitutes, trying to make them feel less than human.

One day while in the trap getting high as fuck, I went broke. A real bad sign for The Tasmanian Devil. So, my higher-than-a-kite gangsta' mentality kicked in and the next thing you know I was beating the shit out of this man and robbing him to get his money.

The beat-down inside ended up outside, all the way down to the corner store on Howard & Tallmadge Ave. When we got there, I knew I had to work fast because I knew the police would soon blow down. I was at it! We squared up and I hit him dead in the nose, busting it wide open. The savage blow knocked him down and out. I snatched his wallet and fled the scene.

I heard my good dude "TT" yell, "Taz, you good? Get in!"

Another homie passing by said, "What's up Taz? You good?"

I replied. "Meet me at the spot (another trap house), Imma need some fire (crack). I'll be there in about 10 minutes."

I was loaded with cash! TT drove me to Circle K to get some drank. My nerves were bad. At Circle K, I saw my bestie and told her what had happened; then gave her money to go inside Circle K and grab me a couple beers. Shortly thereafter and with beer in hand, I was headed to the dope house.

I arrived at the dope house, rushed inside, and instantly smelled the aroma of crack being smoked.

I couldn't wait to get a pull. After buying dope, and hitting it hard, I got paranoid and started tripping hard. The dope boys wanted me to leave. That triggered my anger once again. So once outside, I started yelling all kinds of bullshit. The neighborhood kids ran up the street hollering, "Taz, Taz."

I said, "What's up?"

They said in unison, "Da' police lookin' for you."

So, I gave each of them a dollar and took off to find the police. Sounds crazy, right? Yeah, well that's how fucked up I was from smoking crack. If there was one thing The Tasmanian Devil couldn't stand, it was having a mothafuckin cop come looking for me. It just pissed me off.

Finally, I found the police and said, "I heard yawl was lookin' for me; here I go!" They pulled up on me talking about, "We just want to question you."

My dumb ass, being all geeked out and shit, blurted out loudly, "Yeah, I did it. I fucked dat nigga up! The pedophile got just what he deserved!"

You guessed it. I was arrested, handcuffed, placed in the cruiser, and hauled off to the Summit County Jail. I would serve a short bid in an orange funky ass jumpsuit and be forced to get clean from the drugs and alcohol I loved so much.

So, there I was locked up in jail, wearing the infamous and unflattering bright orange jumpsuit. I had stuffed a crack pipe between my buttocks (because that's where I kept it when I was on the block). I removed the pipe, took the last hit of cocaine while in the holding cell; then, flushed the pipe down the toilet. Then, I started fussing and cussing about being cut and bleeding.

I had to get a deputy's attention, so I could get a change of clothes. By now I was really high and became agitated. I began banging on the cell door and calling the deputy foul names. After a while, I got tired and gave in to a deep crack induced sleep, bloody orange jumpsuit and all.

The next morning, I went to court. In July 2006, I was convicted of robbery and sentenced to three-to-five years in the penitentiary. However, with a mental illness diagnosis, I served 10 months in the Summit County Jail and was placed on three years of intense probation. I thought, "Damn! That means I will have to drop urine, again."

My probation officer was really cool. "LF" was kind, considerate, and a true professional. Mind you, she didn't take no shit but understood that I needed help. And, I understood that there was no way I could drop clean urine.

· · ·

I was at a place in my life where I lived, and would die, for crack cocaine. I thought, "There is no earthly way in hell for me to be successful with probation for three years."

After dropping urine for an entire month and every last urinalysis was dirty, I was shipped off to IBH Addiction Recovery Center in Portage Lakes, Ohio. Long story short, I was terminated from the program after several months. As it were, I stayed clean of drugs as part of a personal plan and working with my probation officer.

I figured if I stayed clean of drugs on my own after being terminated from rehab, she wouldn't have me locked up for probation violation. It worked. I started going to meetings and working steps with a sponsor, "KJ", who kept me active and we went to meetings together. I was actually living clean and free of drugs.

Also, in 2006, my probation officer referred me to an outpatient treatment program called UMIDOP. I had to drop urine twice a week and I proudly state that I successfully completed the UMIDOP program and had two months left on probation. My mouth watered for the next hit of crack.

That demon was ready to surface once again. Two months later, I was released from probation.

One thing I can say for sure, the two months before release from probation were the most difficult months of my life.

Even though I was staying clean of crack cocaine, I couldn't stop living the fast lifestyle. For example, prostitution was a way of getting fast money. I had regular clients that I called to schedule sex visits.

My clients were generous. I got a cell phone and a car. I thought I was living the life. But what I didn't know was that money was a trigger to my addiction. Once again, my mouth watered for the next hit of crack cocaine.

The crack demon surfaced, once again. I caught a soliciting charge (and drug paraphernalia; 2006 or 2008) and thought, "How am I going to explain this?"

I was found guilty and sentenced to six months in jail. Reality struck: "I couldn't win for losing." I was sick and tired of going to jail. I was just about sick and tired of everything.

CAUGHT SLIPPIN'

*M*ake no mistake, because of the fast lifestyle that I lived in the streets, a catastrophe was bound to happen sooner or later. However, I never thought for a minute that the fast life would one day damn near cost me my life. This is what happened in January 2000:

I had robbed a guy and set up another guy to be robbed. Being guilty of doing this, I can say karma found me and made me pay the piper. I was walking on West Market St and Crosby.

It was cold. I was high and tired from no sleep for several days. A man stopped me and asked for a light. Suddenly, he grabbed my throat and shouted, "Where's the money bitch!"

I couldn't and didn't put up much of a fight.

The man continued choking me. Before unconsciousness, I escaped to a quiet place in my mind and silently prayed, "Dear God, don't let me die like this. Forgive me Lord." That's all I remember before slipping into unconsciousness.

A pastor was alerted of trouble when his dog started barking. At 5:30 a.m., the pastor found me in the snow, partially hidden by a hill. I was scantily dressed.

The pastor called 911. Paramedics arrived and rushed me to Saint Thomas Hospital. I had a faint heartbeat and pulse. Later, I was transported to City Hospital.

The doctors said I was alive because of the amount of alcohol that I had consumed. Imagine that! I was left in the snow to die in sub-zero weather. Alcohol saved my life! I was in a coma for twelve days and hooked up to a respirator. When I regained consciousness, I was told that I would never walk again or use my hands.

While in the Intensive Care Unit, my parents were the only ones permitted to visit me. At some point, my mom whispered in my ear, "Who did this?"

I responded, "I don't know."

My brother, Bodacious, was very upset because

he was not allowed to visit me. I heard him say loudly, "Let me see my sister." I learned later that he was escorted out of the hospital by a security guard.

After being released from City Hospital, I was transported to Edwin Shaw Rehabilitation Center. Initially, I was helpless. Someone else had to feed, dress, and groom me because I couldn't do anything for myself. I couldn't even walk.

I had suffered from a great deal of frostbite. Therapy went very well. The only people that came to see me were my friend "No Sugar", and a few family members.

The Edwin Shaw doctors and therapists worked with me more and more because they called me a miracle waiting to happen. They also said that I was a strong survivor and they weren't going to stop working with me until I could walk.

After nine months of intense therapy, I was feeding myself and walking with difficulty. I was also craving crack cocaine. When released from Edwin Shaw, both hands were completely bandaged.

I was so excited to be leaving Edwin Shaw and had an agenda for the entire day. The first order of business was a store where I could buy a beer. The second stop was a place where I could sell my

Percocet. You guessed it, with money in hand, the third stop was a trap house to buy crack. I was going to make up for lost time.

One of the sickest parts about being a crack cocaine addict is the lengths a person goes through to get high. In my case, both of my hands were completely bandaged; therefore, I couldn't even light my own crack pipe.

Furthermore, I couldn't hold the pipe with my hands for any length of time. So, I tightly held the pipe with my lips pressed hard against it to hold it in place. Boy, was I anxious to get high and meet the other-present-crackheads in La-La Land.

"OOOOHHH shit, I'm on fire!" I yelled. The fire from lighting the pipe had set my bandages on fire. People were laughing. All I can remember is the feeling of that first blast of cocaine.

I was so high, I don't remember who or how the fire was put out. This incident did nothing to stop me. I continued to get high. My crack cocaine addiction continued in full swing for 20+ years. Same shit, different day.

I could honestly say that I was truly sick and tired of dealing with the demon—my addictions. I prayed and prayed. I was ready to change; ready to turn my life around; ready for a new beginning.

Priest finds woman freezing on ground

• Victim not identified, may have been assaulted

BY STEPHANIE WARSMITH
Beacon Journal staff writer

The priest was opening the doors of St. Vincent Catholic Church about 5 a.m. yesterday when he saw a partially clad woman in the snow just outside the church.

The Rev. Joseph Kraker called out to the woman and heard her groan softly. He then ran inside the church and called police.

The woman, described as a black female in her 30s, was suffering from severe hypothermia and frostbite.

She was taken to St. Thomas Hospital, and then later transferred to Akron City Hospital, where she was in serious condition last night.

She did not have any identification, and police so far have been unable to determine who she is.

Police said the woman may have been assaulted. They said it was difficult to determine exactly what happened because of the extent of the woman's exposure.

Kraker said he was not sure if he had ever seen the woman before because he did not get close enough to see her face.

The priest heard a dog barking about 3:30 a.m. He didn't give this another thought, though, until he found the woman.

About 5:15 a.m., Kraker opened

See **FIND,** Page D6

FIND

- Woman is partially hidden by small hill

Continued from Page D1

one of the church doors and then was walking around the outside of the church when he noticed footprints in the snow. He then saw a 10-foot patch of snow that was flattened down, as if there had been a scuffle.

Kraker walked to the front of the church, on the West Market Street side, and saw the woman lying in a grassy patch.

"It was so cold out there, and she didn't have much on," Kraker said.

He thought the woman was dead.

"She wouldn't have stayed there long if she had been alive," he reasoned. But his words to her brought a response.

Kraker, who has been the priest at the church for more than five years, said there are not usually many people around at that time of the morning, especially in the winter. Passers-by might not have been able to see the woman anyway because she was partially hidden by a small hill.

"I don't know how long she'd been there," Kraker said.

Anyone with information about the woman's identity is asked to call the Akron Detective Bureau at 330-375-2490.

CLASSIFIED
Death Notices

Akron Beacon Journal January 28, 2000

AKRON
Woman left in snow talks about attack

A woman found freezing last week outside of an Akron church finally was able to talk to police this week about her attacker.

Cheriese Foster, 26, who police believe to be homeless, was found in the snow outside of St. Vincent Catholic Church on the morning of Jan. 28. She was partially clad, and suffered from severe hypothermia and frostbite.

Police talked to her this week after she was taken off a respirator that was helping her breathe.

Foster told police a man assaulted her outside of the church and left her there.

Police have not made any arrests. Detectives were planning to talk to Foster again last night at Akron City Hospital, where she has been since the attack.

Akron Beacon Journal February 5, 2000

WHY WON'T THE POLICE
BELIEVE ME?

I was raped by a man from out of town. A so-called associate found me and told me a guy with money wanted a girl. He walked me to the truck and the man paid him; the red flag went up instantly.

"Ok! Where's my money?" I asked.

The guy replied, "You're already paid for."

I went for the door but there was no handle. I struggled with this 270+ pound man and lost. My pride wasn't hurt because at the time I didn't have any. I was angry because I was taken against my will, got played like a broken violin, and still came out broke.

I ran to my best friend "Ty" and we walked to St. Thomas Hospital where I was tested for diseases and a rape kit was done on me. Nothing was done, no follow-up or anything.

The police made a smart-ass remark saying something like, if I wasn't working the streets it would've never happened. Bullshit!

No one deserves to be raped. I am still a human being. I have rights. A prostitute even has rights. Money for goods; no money, no goods. A man or woman does not have the right to force themselves on anybody without consent. .... Years later in 2020 Detectives came to my house and said they found the same DNA in another woman.

NORTHSIDE

I was angrier than ever, up and down the streets of Tallmadge and Howard terrorizing the dope boys all because I wanted a hit of crack. All the money I spent with these dudes and they always seemed to fix their mouths to say they were "hurting". In other words, their pockets weren't like they needed them to be.

I used to shout, "If I can't smoke nothin, won't nobody smoke!" This was another way of telling them I was about to act up, make the whole "hood" hot, and put the Northside on radar as a way of shutting it all down. (It was God who kept me alive during these events.)

I went to a certain spot on Vesper and told everyone in the house, it goes down tonight. None of you better be in here if you wanna live. I came back that night and forced everyone who remained in this spot after my fair warning to climb out the back window. Smoke was everywhere and it wasn't crack smoke.

I had set fire to the front porch of the house. A couple dope boys and others did what they had to do to put that one out, not knowing that there would be others that followed. Drug dealers will use you up until you have nothing left to offer but yourself.

Once you're out of money, they will not feed you, buy you a beer, or allow you to take a nap or rest. If it ain't about the money, they will red-button you real quick, have you catching the voicemail until your next come up or payday and then your name is "Auntie" again.

When you walk out of the dope man's life, don't look back and lose his number. Without you, some remain unemployed because 8 outta 10 can't read or write. Some can't even count money unless the money is in all ones or all twenties. No names but this describes one of the most notorious drug dealers on North Hill.

KILLING SPREE

The guy that I spoke on earlier in the book confessed to me of blowing someone's head off from West Akron. I didn't want to hear it. He snorted so much powder he got loose lipped and began telling me in detail how he killed these people and was now on the run.

He trapped me in one of the spots on the Northside, held me at gunpoint, and made me walk with him to his spot. He tortured me until I got fed up, leaped out the window and took off like in my track running days. I escaped death again.

I saw on the news this guy was wanted by police. I didn't know what to do so I stayed in hiding at a friend's house. Eventually I had to come out.

. . .

Dude went to one of my known spots and argued about my whereabouts with a guy I was really close to and ended up shooting and killing him. Omg! Talk about feeling guilt. That hurt me terribly.

I had no choice but to run and tell somebody of his whereabouts but it WASN'T the police. It was his Aunt. She turned him in. It was a big stand off on Royal Place. Police were on the rooftops with sniper guns and all. After his capture, I felt somewhat relieved.

Once again, feeling free, I went on about my spree and got high again. Thanking God for all the wrong things, like allowing me to survive this near death experience and also allowing me to spend the stolen money I had left to go get high.

I was told the guy would do life, after all, he shot and killed two (2) people. I would've been the third if I hadn't escaped. Yes, this nut job was definitely on a killing spree. But I refused to be his next victim.

TESTIMONY: A NEW BEGINNING

*I*n February 2014, I was 41 years old and felt worn out—mentally and physically. Once again, I wanted to give in but didn't know how exactly. I wanted so badly to just die.

It was two days after my birthday and after going "hard in the paint," I decided to pray and just have a one-on-one conversation with God. So, I did. I started praying really hard.

I was no longer afraid nor was I terrified and I remembered (Deuteronomy 31:6 NIV) - Be strong and courageous. Do not be afraid or terrified because of them, for the LORD your God goes with you; he will never leave nor forsake you.

I begged, "Lord, please help me." I also asked forgiveness for all the wrong things I had done and people I had hurt.

A bright, fluorescent-looking light appeared in my apartment; so bright, until it shown right through my midnight blackout curtains. I remember feeling chaotic demons being lifted or escaping from my body. A calmness replaced chaos. I felt different, relieved; but I didn't stop praying. I knew that I had been saved.

I began to cry and said, "Thank you Jesus! Thank you!" I kept saying "Thank you" while rising up from praying knees. And, I kept saying, "Thank you Jesus", while gathering up all drug parapher-nalia and leftover alcohol.

My neighbors probably believed that I had lost my mind, while watching me pour out alcohol and smash crack pipes. No, I hadn't lost my mind, I was delivered by God. He had given me another chance to live life.

The very next day, I called my caseworker and asked to be moved from my neighborhood. I wanted to start over: a new beginning, a fresh start for the new found freedom that I was feeling.

I left furniture and most of my personal belong-ings because I wanted absolutely no material memories of the old crack-addicted me. I honestly felt free at last from crack cocaine addiction.

August 15, 2015, I married Mr. King at Ebenezer Church. He was one of the men from my past that stayed with me through thick and thin, so I thought he was a keeper. He'd been with me through the entire struggle; as a friend, a best friend, and then a husband.

In 2016, I separated from my husband and moved to East Akron to start a whole new life. My past was following me but I truly wanted to be NEW. I was again at peace and happier than ever. I had a new car, a two-bedroom house, my favorite pet, BJ, and I had God. Yes, God was my main accomplishment. Without my faith in him and the grace and mercy He casted upon me, I would never have made it out the trenches of addiction and trauma.

In 2017, I believe God gave me a calling; a purpose which was to reach out to other addicts by telling my story. I have recently, as of December 2020, graduated from Stark State College, earning a certificate in Chemical Dependency so that I can develop the skills necessary to work with addicts, one on one. This is my passion, to reach out to addicts, and pray that someone, somewhere, will be saved from crack cocaine addiction.

I AM MY BROTHER'S KEEPER
(ALCOHOL RELAPSE)

*I*t was 5:38 a.m. when the telephone rang. I answered and received some very disturbing news. News that fucked my head up so bad until I started drinking alcohol, again.

My brother had been shot in the head at his home by a woman named "Beverly", who was a crackhead with priors. At first, I had this huge bubble in my chest and couldn't quite swallow.

This horrible news was so unreal. I fought back tears and rushed to Akron General Hospital. Upon arrival in the lobby, I was told that Ernest James Sherman was not there.

I called around to see if anyone knew anything about the shooting and found out a bunch of jibber jabber that didn't make sense. My brother's roommate explained what happened, but nothing sounded right to me. My brother didn't put his hand on nobody without reason, especially women.

When he had trouble with a woman, he called me to beat her up. I just couldn't understand why this shooting happened. A bunch of all different kinds of stories just didn't add up. I wanted answers and fast! I rode around the neighborhood with vigilante thoughts in my head. I swore to hunt down and destroy the lives of this murdering bitch's relatives.

I started drinking liquor and beer, more and more each day. I became the "demon" from four years earlier. The door previously sealed was now open and Taz came outside.

Taz was, and still is, the monster that lives inside of me and I let him out to avenge my brother's death. I was sick. I couldn't eat, couldn't sleep, had visions, and smelled blood everywhere I went. I lost faith in God. My only question was "why did this have to happen to my brother?"

No answers came. I was on a strict diet of alcoholic beverages. Without eating food, I don't know how I managed to maintain strength. Seventy-two hours later, I believed I was going insane. Something had to give.

During my journey of vengeance, I never actually harmed anyone. Lucky for them. The one and only reason no one was hurt is because I couldn't find anyone in the murderer's family. I actually believed if I had found anyone in her family, I would have felt some type of relief.

I was completely lost that first week. Once again, I wanted to die. I tried turning myself into the psychiatric ward but Community Support Services wouldn't take me. They said I had been drinking alcohol and didn't qualify for admission. Bullshit! I had to get help before I hurt someone including myself.

I bought a gun. I rode and rode looking for the main person who were responsible for my brother's murder. Although Beverly pulled the trigger, "Bobby V" was the initiator. Bobby V told Beverly my brother and his roommate had stolen her handgun.

She left Bobby V, went and got another gun, drove to my brother's house, argued and opened fire on both men. "Kool" was injured, my brother was shot on the side of his head while leaving the room. No the fuck she didn't plead self-defense; it was pre-mediated and done with no mercy and no remorse. I want justice. I will stop at nothing to get just that!

GIVING UP IS NOT AN OPTION

 fter the burial of my brother, I felt some relief. Some weight was lifted off me. I had a 45th birthday coming up, and had to gain some control over my life. I was headed for disaster if I didn't stop drinking alcohol.

I had flashbacks of my life and saw my own death. The day after my birthday I quit drinking again. I hated the monster that I was slowly giving life to again. I had become very mean and disrespectful again. I stopped seeing my daughter. I dropped out of school. I lost weight.

I was determined to get my life back. I had to become the Cheriese my brother would have wanted me to finish being. The Cheriese that he would remind me that he was so proud of. I had to bounce back.

After all was said and done, I had to get on my knees, and ask God to forgive me for blaspheming His name. I cried unto the Lord and He answered. He said I passed my test. I am still grieving but I keep my brother's name alive all around me.

I know he is proud and every now and again he'll even stop by and sit at the foot of my bed. I get goosebumps, but I'm not scared. I know my brother is just checking on me. I knew giving up was not an option and I needed to pray on my relapse.

I am my brother's keeper and he is my protector.

RELATIONSHIPS

J've been in several relationships since I've been clean. I can honestly say they were enjoyable, BUT I'm so emotionally scarred that I doubt that I can ever love again. Men have hurt me beyond measurement.

I'm to the point where now I feel like I've lowered my standards when I started dating active addicts …. Why? Because I believe my mission was to try to save lives. Lives of addicts who still suffer. Men that could fill my void and at the same time I would try to help them.

This is my job and I feel that it's also my calling. But the more I tried helping them, the more I ended up lost and pulled further away from my set goals. I refused to be sexually active in these relationships because sometimes sexual encounters can be emotionally draining and can cause stressful illness. I refuse to commit myself to something so temporary. Relationships, to me, are temporary.

In order for one to love, one must love themselves, and be ready to take on another person's responsibilities. I'm not ready for that. I'm not all the way whole in areas of my life. I have trust issues. Men will try to use you and I have had so much experience with this. I've been used all my life.

When you are coming out of bondage of addiction or trauma and abuse, you CANNOT jump into relationships. I leaped like a frog into many men's arms hoping to find what was lost in me, but instead I found more hurt. My advice to you and for your addiction recovery process is to stay true to yourself and the rest will eventually follow.

Open up your Bible and get a relationship with God. Read His Word and get full of His fruit. God will send whatever you are looking for when He sees fit; even a relationship that's worthy.

WHO IS AN ADDICT?

I am an addict. I used drugs and drugs used me. I became a monster that needed to be tamed and tamed quickly. No love for society, family, friends, or myself.

One thing I must say, even after all I've been through, I'm glad I went through it because my addiction made me who I am today. A leader, a mentor, a caregiver, a mother, a daughter, and a grandmother. I do not regret going through addiction.

I am an ambitious, strong-willed, determined, thoughtful, obedient, respectful, responsible, accountable, goal-seeking, motivated woman today. Yes, I am an addict and proud of my recovery.

MESSAGE TO CURRENT ADDICTS

To all addicts who are suffering, my message to you is "Never give up!" We all fall, and we can all get up with help—you cannot do it alone. You now know most of what I went through to finally get it right. The process of recovery from addiction is not easy. I wanted to recover so badly until I stuck with the program. It does work if you work it.

- Get a sponsor.
- Get some numbers.
- Work on improving self-esteem.
- Join and actively participate in support groups along with recovering addicts with experience, years under their belts.

I never gave up on me and will never give up on you; and neither will the "Man" above. You are worthy. Be the light at the end of your own tunnel. You are the only one who can decide that it's time for a change, and then begin to do something about changing from who you are now to who you can become.

My biggest inspiration came from my best friend. I witnessed her journey to get clean and thought, "If she can do it, so can I." And, I did!

Now I say to suffering addicts, "If I can do it, so can you. I was among the worst crack addicts in Akron, Ohio, but not anymore. Although I have not completed all personal goals, I do feel successful while driving a decent car, living in a decent home, and having a family that stood by me while I was indecent, especially my mom and dad."

RIP MY HOMIES

The subculture family that I experienced for 27+ years as a crack cocaine addict was a relatively close-knit group. Most of the time, we looked out for each other. Besides the lifestyle, we had one other thing in common. We were addicted to the lifestyle in some great form or fashion.

Unfortunately, the lifespan of people in this subculture family is cut short because of murders, accidents, overdoses, and maybe suicides. To former homies who were with me during my struggles and who are no longer on this earth, I know you would be proud of me for kicking the habit and turning my life around.

So, I recognize the following subculture road dogs who are all gone but not forgotten: K.G. "Rabbit", April M., Marky, Markus P., Pig, Pork Chop, Gerald, Tony S., Lady, Lil' brother Rick, Cash, Egypt, last but not least my brother Bodacious, and many others. Rest in peace! I love and miss you ALL!

To my family lost to COVID in 2020, rest easy:
    Aunt Alice
    Aunt Daisy
    Uncle Lawrence
    Uncle Clyde

CONCLUSION

*I*n February 2020, I celebrated six years of being clean from crack cocaine and other mind-altering substances. Yes, I continue to struggle with mental issues but it's nothing that prayer, faith, and meditation can't correct, so I joined a program at Urban Ounce of Prevention, a program for persons with mental health, trauma, and addictions.

One day I plan on applying for employment. It's a beautiful program and all the caseworkers and counselors care about each other and their clients. It's confidential and it works if you work it. They helped me deal with and resolve issues I used to run from, but today I stand and fight each mental battle like a champion.

. . .

As of the completion of this book, I graduated from Stark State College, maintaining a 3.8 GPA. I was awarded several distinctions.; one being the President's List of Spring 2019, the Dean's List of Fall 2019, and again the President's list of Spring and Fall 2020. I'm currently employed doing what I love best which is working with the addicted at Legacy 3 located in Akron, Ohio.

I am still awaiting justice for my brother's murder and hope the sentencing will be granted in 2020. All I can do is continue to let go and let God.

I still suffer from PTSD, anxiety, and some paranoia. That's due to the traumatic things that happened to me during my childhood and my addiction. But I'm alive and well due to the many medications I take on a daily basis and GOD, of course.

I am still a client, reaching out to clients, but guess what? Who would make a better candidate to assist others in recovery and trauma than myself.

I qualify in all areas and I plan on giving back to my community. These long few years in college are what led me to understand that counseling and supporting my peers are what needs to be done. This is my calling.

God willing and keeping Him first, this is exactly what I will retire doing. I believe in myself and I believe in all who have suffered and are still suffering from mental illness, abuse and addiction.

Look at me now! I am proud, ambitious, goal seeking, caring and today I can live again. Let's stand strong together. You can be anything you put your mind to doing. I am a walking testimony. I survived.

Ohio Chemical Dependency Professionals Board

CERTIFIES THAT

Cheriese Marcel Foster

HAVING GIVEN EVIDENCE OF COMPETENCY AND DEMONSTRATION OF REQUIRED KNOWLEDGE AND SKILLS AND HAVING MET ALL CRITERIA IN ACCORDANCE WITH ALL APPROVED STANDARDS AND PROCEDURES ESTABLISHED BY THE BOARD HEREBY CONFERS AND AUTHORIZES THE USE OF THE DESIGNATED CREDENTIAL

Chemical Dependency Counselor Assistant Preliminary

IN WITNESS WHEREOF THE SEAL AND SIGNATURES OF THE BOARD ARE HEREUNTO AFFIXED.

Chair

Vice Chair

Executive Director

Issue Date   8/15/2020

Credential No.   CDCA 174329

STARK STATE COLLEGE

HEALTH AND PUBLIC SERVICES DIVISION

This is to certify that

CHERIESE MARCEL FOSTER

Having satisfactorily completed all credit requirements of instruction is awarded the

CAREER ENHANCEMENT CERTIFICATE
IN CHEMICAL DEPENDENCY
DECEMBER 20, 2020

Cheriese Foster, a survivor of drugs and alcohol has now made it her mission in life to give back to her community. Her passion and purpose in life is to help the addicted. She struggled with 27 years of drug abuse of crack cocaine  and alcohol until she had a spiritual awakening where The God of her understanding showed up and showed out. She made a complete 180!

Cheriese, a wife, mother, and grandmother, is a graduate of Stark State College majoring in Chemical Dependency, maintaining a 3.85 GPA as of December 2020. She received three certificates with one being the President's List of Spring 2019, Dean's List of Fall 2019, and lastly, a Taylor My Heart Award during the Strides Of Strength Gala 2019, accompanied by Akron councilwoman Tara

Samples. Cheriese received an online diploma in 2016 at age 41.

She has a favorite rescue-animal named BJ. She enjoys mentoring children, giving them hope to speak up and be their own voice, and speaking inside the rooms of AA, so hopefully her story about her own past drug addiction will one day help someone else to recover.

This powerful, motivated, God-fearing woman has a story to tell.

AFTERWORD

I have developed a criminal record that I am not proud of, but I am also writing this book to express my deepest apologies for these acts of unruliness.

At the time that all these crimes were committed, I was involved in chronic addiction to alcohol and other drugs. I realize that drug and alcohol abuse can destroy a person's past, but I'm asking that society not allow it to destroy my future by holding it against me.

I'm trying to earn a chance to right my wrongs and be able to help adolescents and adults who suffer from substance abuse and other issues. I am a positive role model in my community and also a law abiding citizen today. I take my career of Chemical Dependency and Human Social Services seriously.

I know I can help make a difference in the lives of persons with addictions.

REFERENCE

http://encyclopedia.uia.org/en/problem/148022